YAS

P9-BIV-010

The Girls' Book of Love

COOL QUOTES, SUPER
STORIES, AWESOME ADVICE,
AND MORE

Edited by Catherine Dee

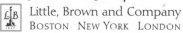

Megan Tingley Books

Little, Brown and Company
BOSTON   NEW YORK   LONDON

To Prince Rumpis

Compilation copyright © 2002 by Catherine Dee
Illustrations copyright © 2002 by Ali Douglass

All rights reserved. No part of this book may be reproduced in any form or by any electronic or mechanical means, including information storage and retrieval systems, without permission in writing from the publisher, except by a reviewer who may quote brief passages in a review.

First Edition

Library of Congress Cataloging-in-Publication Data
The girls' book of love : cool quotes, super stories, awesome advice, and more / edited by Catherine Dee.
p. cm.
Summary: A collection of true stories, quotes, poems, and personal advice on various aspects of romantic relationships and being in love.
ISBN 0-316-17404-1
1. Love—Miscellanea—Juvenile literature. 2. Man-woman relationships—Miscellanea—Juvenile literature. 3. Interpersonal relations in adolescence—Miscellanea—Juvenile literature. [1. Love—Miscellanea. 2. Interpersonal relations—Miscellanea.] I. Dee, Catherine.
HQ801 .G468 2002
306.7—dc21   2002019108

10 9 8 7 6 5 4 3 2 1

Acknowledgments

This book seems to have magically materialized thanks to all the girls and women who provided love stories, poems, and quotes. Thanks to Elizabeth Carlassare and Sarah Dee for excellent feedback and to Jeanie Fraser for research help. Heaps of appreciation to Alana Webb of lovestories.com, Nancy Gruver of *New Moon*, and Rivka Solomon and Julia DeVillers, who publicized my call for material. The biggest thanks of all to Megan Tingley for making this series possible, along with my patient editor, Mary Gruetzke, and the team at Little, Brown: Kerri Goddard Kinch, Linda Magram, Alvina Ling, and Will Gordon. A big hug to my wonderful husband, Jonathan Ganz, whom I had the pleasure of marrying while working on this book. Finally, a toast to my incredible family: Mom, Dad, Vicky, Sarah, Ryan, Dick, Hal, Charley, Mike, Jessie, Jeremy, Jack, and Ben—the people I love most in the world.

Contents

Introduction

Welcome to *The Girls' Book of Love*. I'm glad to be able to provide you with this collection of quotes, stories, poems, song lyrics, and facts to help deepen your understanding of love. The women and girls in this book have been in love. They've felt the exhilaration of crushes and lived through the disappointment of rejection; they've ridden the whole roller coaster of relating. Along the way they've learned what works, what doesn't, and when to let a relationship go. They know the difference between infatuation and a deep connection. They know what lasting love requires, and what it gives back. And they're happy to share this all with you!

When I was a teen, I was pretty clueless about romantic relationships. After flipping through ads in magazines and seeing television shows, I thought that love was essentially a blissful, floaty sensation. (Sometimes it is . . . but there is so much more.) If I had known then what I do now about real-life love, I would have been better prepared and had different expectations. So I hope this book will do that for you: shine a light on the mysteries of love and give you an idea of the possibilities.

The Girls' Book of Love focuses on the emotions surrounding the pursuit of romantic connections. It's not meant to help you snag a boyfriend or learn how to flirt but to give you a greater appreciation for what love is and how it might affect you. It's a celebration of love balanced out by a little practical advice and some reality checking. It's intended to give you a glimpse into the intense feelings of having a crush, the letdown of being attracted to someone who doesn't like you back, the comfort of being with a long-term sweetie. This book is an optimistic yet realistic picture of what love could hold as you explore it in the months and years ahead.

Each chapter includes a mix of several elements, including:

Cool Quotes. Let the actors, singers, writers, and other women and girls quoted at the beginning of each chapter enlighten you on everything from first dates to soulmates. Need a little wisdom on "just being friends" or how to cope with being dumped? Just flip to the right chapter for some comforting thoughts.

Guy's-Eye View. Wonder how boys and men feel about love, and whether they see things as you do? This section presents some profound, sappy, and entertaining reflections from the other half of the population.

True Stories. Once you've read some quotes, delve into a few true tales. This section features stories about asking guys out, taking drivers' training with a crush, and more. Some of these stories will give you a warm fuzzy feeling, while others will get you thinking: "Could that happen to me?" or "How would I feel in that situation?"

Love Poems. For some reason, being in love makes people want to write poetry. The poems in this section express devotion, what it feels like to be crazy for someone, disappointment, and more.

Romantic Lyrics. You've probably heard hundreds of songs about love. Read here for some of the best love lyrics written or sung by women.

Quick Lists. Check out this section for love data such as girls' favorite romantic movies and good places to go on dates.

FASCINATING FACTS. These survey findings, trends, and trivia about love are waiting for you at the end of most of the chapters.

Whether you're new to the notion of love or into the nuts and bolts of dating and relating, I hope *The Girls' Book of Love* will be a help to you. I hope it inspires you to reach for love's highest heights and empowers you to embark upon the road to true love with a clear understanding and great expectations!

Catherine Dee

Chapter 1

Crazy Little Thing

 The word "love"—as in the romantic kind—brings to mind crazy crushes and sweet kisses, mushy valentines and cozy snuggling. But what exactly *is* love?

Some people think it's the experience of being instantly smitten with someone. Others believe it's a state of caring that develops between two people over the years. Some see it as a deeper shade of friendship, unconditional regard for another, or the willingness to protect the person from harm at all costs.

As you can see, trying to fit love into one handy definition is a challenge. That's okay, because in order to really understand it, you've got to experience it.

Cool Quotes

The sweetest joy, the wildest woe is love.
> —PEARL BAILEY, ENTERTAINER, 1918–1990

Love is the one experience of the human condition that allows us to feel unequivocally, beautifully, and deeply that our true condition is not isolation but union.
> —DAPHNE ROSE KINGMA, WRITER

Love is the most important thing in life. If you don't have [a relationship], you're always looking for one.
> —SHERYL CROW, SINGER-SONGWRITER

Love is coming face to face with the knowledge that you've found the best friend you'll ever have in this world.
> —LUCY MURRAY, ARTIST, WRITER

Love is the vital essence that pervades and permeates, from the center to the circumference, the graduating circles of all thought and action.

—ELIZABETH CADY STANTON, SUFFRAGIST,
WRITER, SOCIAL REFORMER, 1815–1902

Love, in my opinion, is not a fantasy, not the stuff of romance novels or fairy tales. It's as gritty and real as the subway, it comes around just as regularly, and as long as you can stick it out on the platform, you won't miss it.

—LOIS SMITH BRADY, WRITER

[Love] is perhaps the only glimpse we are permitted of eternity.

—HELEN HAYES, ACTOR, 1900–1993

Love is everything it's cracked up to be. . . . It really is worth fighting for, being brave for, risking everything for.

—ERICA JONG, WRITER

Guy's-Eye View

What Is Love? I have met in the streets a very poor young man who was in love. His hat was old, his coat worn, the water passed through his shoes and the stars through his soul.

—VICTOR HUGO, WRITER, 1802–1885

True Story
Matchmaker Moms & Dads

When my parents met some friends at a party and found out that they had a son living near me, they practically turned cartwheels. The children's numbers were exchanged while we, the children, remained unaware that our parents had changed the course of our lives.

The first time he and I spoke on the phone, we talked for hours. He asked what long-term plans I had (not many). I asked how many pierces and tattoos he had ("What?!"). By the end of the conversation, I knew at the very least that I had made a friend. And friendship became love.

Now it's hard to imagine life without each other. We often wonder what would have happened if there had been no party where our parents could meet, no friendship between them. We have a favorite Hebrew saying, "B'shert"—*Meant to be.* Even if our parents had never met, even if our lives had taken different paths, I believe we were b'shert, and sooner or later, our paths would have crossed.

—JENNIFER BERNSTEIN-LEWIS, VOLUNTEER COORDINATOR

Chapter 2

All You Need Is Love

Romantic love is powerful. It's the driving force behind our very existence—each new generation owes itself to the couples who fall in love, marry, and start families. With its promises of erasing loneliness and making us feel cherished, true love is most everyone's deepest wish.

Lovestruck couples are full of energy, which can lead them to accomplish great feats, either in the name of love or as a side effect. People in love also have the capacity to learn and do things together that they wouldn't do alone.

Love won't solve all your problems. If you don't have a life, love won't give you one. Short of that, never underestimate the power. . . .

Cool Quotes

Love conquers all things except poverty and a toothache.

—MAE WEST, ACTOR, 1893–1980

I don't want to live. I want to love first, and live incidentally.

—ZELDA FITZGERALD, WRITER, 1900–1948

Intimate relationships cannot substitute for a life plan. But to have any meaning or viability at all, a life plan must include intimate relationships.

—HARRIET LERNER, PSYCHOLOGIST, WRITER

The love of my true companion makes me rich beyond anything material a man could ever give to me.

—BARBARA DEANGELIS, WRITER, SPEAKER

Love—an inaccessible dream or a contingent reality—is undeniably as essential to us as the air we breathe.

—MONIQUE PIVOT, WRITER

Being in love and being loved keep you young.

—MADONNA, SINGER

Guy's-Eye View

The meeting of two personalities is like the contact of two chemical substances; if there is any reaction, both are transformed.

—CARL JUNG, PSYCHOANALYST, 1875–1961

True Story
Sneaking Up on Love

It happened in Alexandria, a gorgeous Egyptian city on the sea with a divine blend of soothing water and penetrating sunsets. My cousin and I were walking along one night when I saw this guy in front of us who took my breath away, even though I was looking at his *back*. I had to catch a glimpse of his face, so I grabbed my cousin and walked toward him. When he turned around and looked at me, it felt like a thousand leeches were pressing against my heart, sucking out every drop of energy and sanity I possessed. His eyes were flecked with specks of yellow amidst a sea of glorious green. I just froze.

The attraction was mutual. In the coming days we spent long hours together, sitting and talking on a big boulder on the beach. In his arms, my heart and his seemed to beat as one, and I felt weightless and so right.

Although our time together was short, it's a treasure I'll hold in my heart forever. He was the beginning of something great, and through his eyes I saw the beauty of life.

—DINA CHEHATA, 16

Chapter 3

The Crush Rush

 You know you've entered the world of love when you get a crush on someone. Twelve-year-old Catherine Vogt sums up what it feels like: "All I want is for him to feel the same way about me. I get butterflies in my stomach and my palms sweat. I try to look better to get his attention. I would talk to him, but the words won't come. I would give him my soul and my life."

Regardless of their outcomes, crushes make you feel *alive*. If they turn into real dating, something is lost. So savor all crushing, whether you're simply adoring the person of your dreams *in* your dreams or moving toward saying hi and discovering if the feeling is mutual.

Cool Quotes

The absolute yearning of one human body for another particular one and its indifference to substitutes is one of life's major mysteries.

—IRIS MURDOCH, WRITER, 1919–1999

Tiny, little needles being pricked into your skin all over your body. What *is* this? . . . You are demonstrating classic symptoms of *chrushus amorus*.

—SARI LOCKER, ADVICE COLUMNIST

More than anything in this transitory life mine eyes desire the sight of you.

—CATHERINE OF ARAGON, QUEEN OF ENGLAND,
1485–1536, IN A LETTER TO HENRY VIII

Sometimes I'll get a glimpse of him and think, "Hey, that guy is really cute." You feel a physical change when you see the man you love.

—MARLO THOMAS, ACTOR, ACTIVIST

The mark of a true crush . . . is that you fall in love first and grope for reasons afterward.

—SHANA ALEXANDER, WRITER

True Story
A Good Sport

Tim was a senior on the varsity swim team with my friend Kelly's brother, so Kelly and I went to swim meets together. We sat with Tim's girlfriend, Linda. I didn't have enough self-confidence to talk to Tim, and when he talked to Kelly and Linda, my face turned bright red and I got so nervous that I couldn't say a word. I was jealous when he held Linda's hand. She acted like having Tim as a boyfriend was no big deal, and I couldn't understand that.

Never in a million years did I think Tim and I would get together, but during the last week of school he broke up with Linda. Apparently he had been noticing me the whole time I'd been noticing him, and a few days later he asked me out.

I was afraid I'd make a fool of myself, but everything went great. I still remember the electricity that shot through my body when he reached over and held my hand during the movie. At the end of the night he kissed me. It was magic.

That summer we spent every day together, holding hands, laughing, and being in love. Although our relationship didn't survive the strain of his going away to college, he'll always hold a special place in my heart.

— JULIE NIECE, CONSTRUCTION COMPANY ASSISTANT

FASCINATING FACTS

Fantasies—such as those swooning thoughts about your crush—are so powerful that they may act as a natural pain reliever, according to the American Pain Society.

Want to know if your crush likes you without revealing your interest? A little undercover sleuthing could be in order. If you have an e-mail address and know your crush's e-mail address, go to eCrush *(http://www. ecrush.com/)*. While you're there, check out all the fabulous features on this site, from dating horror stories and pickup lines to the e-mail address of your celebrity crush.

Chapter 4

Just One Look

Have you ever fallen in love at first sight?

Maybe you spotted a gorgeous hunk and your legs turned to Jell-O, or you heard elevator music and just knew, deep inside, that this was It. Maybe it really was instant love that will last a lifetime (sigh).

There is, however, a large chance that this type of lightning-bolt experience is something else at first sight: infatuation. Generally, true love is thought to develop over time. But infatuation can certainly lead to love.

Either way, it's not every day that you fall for a stranger in the blink of an eye. Get ready, because when you do, your life will never be the same.

Cool Quotes

You know when people say, "He turned my head"? My head spun around on my body! Not many people stop you in your tracks.

—MADONNA, SINGER, ON MEETING HUSBAND GUY RITCHIE

No one knows how it is that with one glance a boy can break through into a girl's heart.

—NANCY THAYER, WRITER

Love is like a virus. It can happen to anybody at any time.

—MAYA ANGELOU, POET, WRITER

Love at first sight is the ultimate gut instinct.

—LOIS SMITH BRADY, WRITER

I do [believe in love at first sight]. But I also believe in, "How do you keep it going?"

— DREW BARRYMORE, ACTOR

Guy's-Eye View

You've got to keep the faith. Who doesn't like the idea that you could see someone tomorrow and she could be the love of your life?

— LEONARDO DiCAPRIO, ACTOR

Love at first sight is a kind of peaceful death. There's utter silence, and a light that radiates pure warmth. When you next open your eyes, the world is a new place; you've only begun to be alive.

— JASON ALLEN WISE, STUDENT

I knew from the minute I saw her that if I got involved with her I would fall in love with her.

— BILL CLINTON, FORMER U.S. PRESIDENT, ON WIFE, HILLARY

True Stories
A Gift from the Gods

As a sixteen-year-old visiting temples in India with my family, I suddenly felt someone's intense gaze. When I looked up to see him standing a stone's throw away, our eyes locked.

He was tall and handsome, with a head full of fresh black curls and a slight razor stubble shadowing his cheeks. His eyes had the calmness of the deep sea and the forcefulness of the waves. Soon I was staring at him as shamelessly as he was at me. He didn't say a word, but warmth flooded between us. The wind whispered, "He is the seventh color of your rainbow."

I had surely found my Mr. Right, but then he began walking away. I panicked but moved with my family in the opposite direction. He looked back and smiled a gentle, knowing smile.

And there ends this love story, if I may call it one. Years have passed, and I have gone on with my life. We may never meet again, but a strange happiness comes over me when my mind strays to him. This astounding man gave me a gift—a sense of knowledge that sustains me. Nothing really happened, but in that nothingness there's a strange contentment. That's the way it is with love—it is complete in and of itself; it seeks no other fulfillment.

—KAMALIKA BARAL, STUDENT

Snow White and the Seven Years

As soon as we saw one another, I was done for. I knew straightaway that I'd met "him." I really felt like Snow White being taken out of the glass coffin.

But first, we had a lot of yelling to do. I mean that in a good way. We are both intense people, and initially we bumped up against each other, challenging each other on a lot of levels. We didn't hide anything emotionally. Now, nearly seven years down the road, we don't look back like some couples and say, "Oh, how lovely it was at the beginning." For us, it was really tough at first, and now it's much richer and better. We did it backward.

—KATE BECKINSALE, ACTOR, FROM *PARADE*

FASCINATING FACT

According to a Knight Ridder Survey, twenty-five percent of Americans say love at first sight is a Hollywood fantasy, but sixty-five percent believe in it.

Chapter 5

Love Signs

 How do you know you're in love?

Congratulations if you just *know*. But don't feel bad if there are no bells and whistles and you'd feel weird proclaiming, "I'M IN LOVE!" Or if you love someone but aren't sure you're *in* love. The defining moment doesn't necessarily flash like a neon sign; it may show in more subtle ways.

If you're in love-identification limbo, be patient. You can't order your heart to make a statement. It will tell you when it's good and ready. In time, the nature of your connection will become clear, and you'll know that either you've misjudged the romantic possibilities (no big deal) or that you're certifiably head over heels.

Cool Quotes

If only one could tell true love from false love as one can tell mushrooms from toadstools.
—KATHERINE MANSFIELD, WRITER, 1888–1923

I knew after that first date. It's that thing—you just know when you know.
—TÉA LEONI, ACTOR

You know when you're in love because as soon as they leave, you already miss them. Things that may have been a turnoff before are cute and funny.
—SARAH MAURICE, COLLEGE STUDENT

There's some modern truth to Cinderella's tale—it's love when you're incredibly comfortable, when the shoe fits perfectly.
—LOIS SMITH BRADY, WRITER

You know when it's easy. When it doesn't feel like work. . . . You know it's love when it all just kind of falls into place.

—LINDSAY SLOANE, ACTOR

When you are in love with someone, you want to be near him all the time, except when you are out buying things and charging them to him.

—MISS PIGGY, MUPPET

Be honest with yourself. . . . You *do* know within the first few minutes of a date whether you can actually see him in your life picture.

—CYNTHIA GARRET, TV SHOW HOST

When you love someone, all your saved-up wishes start coming out.

—ELIZABETH BOWEN, WRITER, 1899–1973

Guy's-Eye View

When I fell in love with Yoko, I knew, my God, this is different from anything I've ever known. . . . This is more than a hit record, more than gold, more than everything.
—JOHN LENNON, MUSICIAN, 1940–1980

You walk into a strange room. It's not of your design, but you feel instantly at home. Somehow another person has arranged the order of things so that you fit. That was the experience of meeting [my wife] Judith.
—BILL MOYERS, TV JOURNALIST

True Stories
The Art of Knowing

I felt intensely about Jeff, a decent seventeen-year-old with a few problems. I liked him tremendously; I wanted to be with him all the time. I was attracted to him. I was interested in everything he had to say. But I wasn't in that altered state of consciousness that I thought of as being "in love." What I felt about him didn't match what I saw in the movies or read in books.

A few years later, I *truly* fell in love, with Jon, the best-looking guy I've ever met. And he was interested in me! I wanted to climb the nearest mountain and shout it from the summit: "I'm in love!" I hardly ate. I was obsessed. I had no doubt that I'd met Mr. Right. I started fantasizing about marriage and babies.

But then he started acting different. And when I finally got him to admit something had changed, he said: "Feelings come and go. That's the way they are. I just don't *feel* it anymore."

One thing that helped me get over Jon was reading *The Art of Loving* by Erich Fromm. It says that real love—

as opposed to that heady, movie-type feeling—is care, responsibility, respect, and knowledge. In other words, you can only really love someone you know. And that takes time. It means finding out about a person, hanging out for a while, watching them in action in all kinds of situations.

I now realize that I was all wrong: With Jon it was a great experience that I don't regret for a second, but it wasn't love. And with Jeff, even though I wasn't flying high, it was love.

—TAMRA DAWN, WRITER, FROM WHOLEFAMILY.COM

Checking Him Out

When I was 15, I knew the kind of man I was going to marry. Serious and literate—maybe an English professor. Tall, with a mustache, driving a VW Bug, and loving to stay up late talking about books. I always kept this image in the back of my mind as a sort of yardstick.

Then I met Bud. He loved to tell really corny jokes, he was clean-cut with short hair, he drove his father's station wagon, and he seldom read books. To top it off, he was a part-time math teacher. Our first date was a trip to the grocery store, and, believe it or not, it was fun. I put weird food in his cart, and he told me about strange meals his mother served. I knew he was the one for me when we went through the checkout lane: He had to fill out an application for a check-cashing card, and he got red in the face and began to sweat.

We've been together ever since, and we still have fun grocery shopping!

—ELLEN BIRKETT MORRIS, WRITER

FASCINATING FACTS

Heady stuff: A German scientist studied the brain waves of college students who claimed to be "truly and madly in love." Looking at photos of their beloveds produced a certain brain-wave pattern. His conclusion? There could be a scientific way to measure love.

According to *Psychology Today*, thirty-five percent of the people in a survey said they knew they were in love because they worried about their "friend." Twenty-seven percent knew it was love when they laughed at the same joke.

Chapter 6

Falling for You

 We talk about love as "falling" because it involves an element of surrender: You can't control when, where, or with whom you'll be in love. People bitten by the lovebug also seem to "lose it" and become suddenly blind to practical things, such as whether the person is compatible or a good bet for a relationship.

Landing in a relationship could be compared to going on a free-fall amusement-park ride. You can see it coming, but you are helpless to stop the fall. When it happens, it's nothing short of exhilarating. At some point you come back to earth—either via a crash or a gentle landing—and get back in line for another spin.

Cool Quotes

Why do fools fall in love? It's simple: because it feels good and they don't know any better.

—PATRICIA LOVE, EDUCATOR, SPEAKER, RELATIONSHIP CONSULTANT

Falling in love consists merely in uncorking the imagination and bottling the common sense.

—HELEN ROWLAND, JOURNALIST, 1875–1950

If it is your time, love will track you down. . . . If you say, "No! I don't want it right now," that's when you'll get it for sure.

—LYNDA BARRY, CARTOONIST

Before I met my husband I'd never fallen in love, though I'd stepped in it a few times.

—RITA RUDNER, COMEDIAN

Enjoy the fall. . . . Thrill to the sensation of air rushing past as the pavement approaches and you suddenly discover—though you're not sure how—that you've . . . *sprouted wings!*

—CHRISTINE SCHULTZ, EDITOR, WRITER

Guy's-Eye View

It's hard to describe why it is, that "click," why it is two people become infatuated with each other and then fall in love. It didn't take me long. . . . In many ways it was just a couple of days.

—GEORGE W. BUSH, U.S. PRESIDENT, ABOUT HIS WIFE, LAURA

True Story
Puppy Love

My sister Kacie gave me an odd look as I stroked her puppy and said I thought it was cute.

"You've never uttered the word 'cute' without attaching a sarcastic comment," she said. "I expected you to kick that puppy, not pet it!"

She was right. I'd been the most cynical person on earth.

"I'm just excited because I have a new boyfriend. When the novelty wears off I'll return to normal," I said, trying to convince myself.

I had never believed in love. Jared was the reason I'd sworn off of males. Frightened of criticism and a broken heart, I had vowed to never like another boy, but then Matt ruined my plans. Fate brought us together at a party. We met outside under the stars and talked until dawn; it was as if we'd know each other forever. When we went to a baseball game on our first date, he made me forget that I knew nothing about baseball. We spent the entire afternoon talking, laughing, and stuffing our faces with hot dogs and nachos.

"Hello? Earth to Kristin?" said Kacie. "It's okay. Let yourself love him; you deserve it."

A giant smile spread across my face. I'd discovered love! Giggling, I grabbed my sister's hand and sprinted after her fluffy yellow dog.

—KRISTIN BLUHM, STUDENT

Romantic Lyrics

i'm sorry i can't help you, i cannot keep you safe
i'm sorry i can't help myself, so don't look at me
   that way

we can't fight gravity on a planet that insists
that love is like falling
and falling is like this.

—ANI DiFRANCO, SINGER-SONGWRITER

FASCINATING FACTS

Who falls in love first—the guy or the girl? According to psychologist Joyce Brothers, researchers have found that a quarter of men fall in love before the fourth date, compared with only fifteen percent of women.

In a *Twist* magazine poll, thirty-three percent of the girl respondents said they were in love, and twenty percent had been in love before. Twenty-seven percent said they hadn't fallen in love yet, and another twenty percent said they weren't sure.

Chapter 7

First Love

 Think back to the first time you rode a bike or went to school. It was a little scary, but once you dove in, you had a great time. Remember the thrill you felt as you were initiated into these grand new adventures?

It's the same with first love, only the thrill can be more intense. Your first romance is like nothing you've ever known or can really imagine, no matter what your big sister or aunt has told you about love. It's also significant because you approach it without preconceptions. The experience leaves you with "baseline" knowledge of love, as if you're a piece of clay that's been imprinted.

May your first love leave a wonderful imprint on your life.

Cool Quotes

When first we fall in love, we feel that we know all there is to know about life, and perhaps we are right.

— MIGNON MCLAUGHLIN, WRITER

I will always remember how he was my first boyfriend, and all the things I felt *because* of him.

— NICOLE SYNGAJEWSKI, 15

You can remember the second and the third and the fourth time, but there is no time like the first. It's always there.

— SHELAGH DELANEY, PLAYWRIGHT

I'm glad it cannot happen twice, the fever of first love.

— DAPHNE DU MAURIER, WRITER, 1907–1989

I had my first love, and it was something so incredible and indescribable that I will treasure it always.

—KATIE HOLMES, ACTOR

Guy's-Eye View

The magic of first love is our ignorance that it can ever end.

—BENJAMIN DISRAELI, PRIME MINISTER
OF GREAT BRITAIN, 1804–1881

True Stories
Special Delivery

I was fifteen when I first fell in love. Bernard was sixteen and came from Boston to Ontario, Canada, to spend the summer with his grandmother, who lived on the farm next to ours. He was tall and slim, with sparkling blue eyes and blond, wavy hair. He made me feel special, and we spent a lot of time together before he went home.

On February 14, the postman knocked on the door with a package for me. I was so excited that I could hardly breathe as I opened the large, red, heart-shaped box. It was filled with candy that said *Be my valentine* and *Will you be mine?* I ran up to my room to read the sayings away from my brother, who thought it was funny.

No gift since has thrilled me like that valentine from my first love.

—MURIEL CALEGARI, WRITER

For Better or Worse

My first love, Jimmy, and I had been an item since seventh grade, and after an on-again, off-again relationship in high school, we went to the senior ball. The night ended at a dawn beach party. We came to my house long enough to change clothes before breakfast when the phone rang. My favorite grandmother had just died.

Without hesitating, Jimmy got in the car and drove my mother and me six hours to the waiting relatives. He attended the funeral and was a constant support for my whole family, and especially me.

Jimmy and I decided to go our separate ways in college. But I will forever cherish the memory of his being there for me after the ball.

—ALDEN (BOBBI) DEAN, POET

FASCINATING FACT

A *New York Times* survey found that fifty-nine percent of people still think about their first teenage love.

Chapter 8

In Your Dreams

 Your dream guy is a mega movie star or the leader of a pop rock band. Or maybe he's just a figment of your imagination—someone with the perfect blend of physical features, personality, and interests—including, of course, interest in you. The two of you would "complete" each other, you would never argue, and, like in the movies, you'd ride off into the sunset.

Dreaming is fun, but it helps to keep dreams in perspective. Keep one eye out for a real-life prince, "warts and all." Of course he won't measure up to your fantasy version, but he'll be more likely to have one thing going for him: *availability!*

Cool Quotes

Before we love with our heart, we already love with our imagination.

—LOUISE COLET, POET, WRITER, 1810–1876

You want a prince, you want Jesus. So when he comes around and his name is, like, Steve, what are you supposed to do?

—MACY GRAY, SINGER

My mom never taught me to be waiting for some prince on a white horse to swipe me off my feet.

—TYRA BANKS, MODEL

Love a man for who he is right now, not for his potential.

—JANET PLUSH, PARALEGAL

I thought relationships were these . . . experiences where you get carried away with someone. . . . But once I experienced that often enough, I didn't want to have anything to do with it.

— ALANIS MORISSETTE, SINGER-SONGWRITER

True Story
A Sweet Story

When I was younger, I thought all I needed to have the boyfriend of my dreams was to lose ten pounds. Even when I was older and more comfortable with the body I was given, I thought that if I tried hard enough to demonstrate self-confidence and awareness, a man would appear. He would know I deserved everything I wanted, and he'd put all of his needs aside to make sure I got it.

I discovered that love is nothing like the motion-picture version, where men are wonderfully sensitive and walk the earth only to make true love last forever with *you*—a beautiful, thin, rich, and exotic woman.

Love is about making compromises and being flexible. It requires a tireless effort to understand each other when you're confused, and to have faith in one another when you're full of doubt. If it were as easy as riding a bike, it would get old and you would outgrow it. If it were all about finding someone to make you happy, you would never be happy enough.

But loving someone day to day is wonderful—better than a triple chocolate brownie with whipped cream and sprinkles. Because unlike a heavenly dessert, love lasts from one day to the next. It never leaves you hungry for more, and there's no limit to how much you can give or receive. And the best part is that you get to share life with your best friend, which can turn even sourgrape days into a delicious sundae.

—NANCY MACGREGOR, PUBLIC RELATIONS CONSULTANT

Quick List: Romantic Faves

When asked to name their favorite love movie, girls in an informal Web survey said:

As Good as It Gets

Chocolat

Circle of Friends

Down to You

Ever After: A Cinderella Story

Ghost

Grease

Here on Earth

Hope Floats

Love and Basketball

Message in a Bottle

Never Been Kissed

Notting Hill

Romeo and Juliet

Runaway Bride

Save the Last Dance

Sleepless in Seattle

The Sound of Music

Ten Things I Hate About You

Titanic

West Side Story

You've Got Mail

Chapter 9

Making Your Move

 You've had your eye on him for months. You know his routine, where you're most likely to run into him, and other assorted tidbits. You pine away for him and hope someday he'll notice you.

Why not take matters into your own hands? It can be scary to expose your feelings instead of playing it cool, and you may be turned down. But life is short. If you don't ask, you'll never know if he's interested, and you could miss out on a great relationship.

If you're turned down, it will be disappointing, but a "no" won't ruin your life. "So you feel like a doof," says advice columnist Carolyn Hax. "How will you feel ten years from now if you never even tried?"

Cool Quotes

I marched straight up to him and said, "So I hear you have a crush on me." We've been together ever since.

—ROSE McGOWAN, ACTOR

I've always been the pursuer. If I didn't, they would assume I wouldn't go out with them, and I would still be completely alone.

—BROOKE SHIELDS, ACTOR

I kept watching him the whole time, waiting for him to make the first move. He didn't. So I asked him if he wanted to get some coffee, and he said yes.

—ELISABETH SHUE, ACTOR

The craziest thing I did to get a guy to notice me was when I ripped his favorite old T-shirt and promptly got nachos smushed in my hair.

—MOLLY RINGWALD, ACTOR

When I was doing [a movie], I didn't have anyone to go to opening night with. Finally I got up the courage to say to [a carpenter on the set], "I was wondering if, um, you would consider going out to dinner sometime." He looked at me and said, "In a heartbeat."

—GLENN CLOSE, ACTOR

Guy's-Eye View

Show up and take me out to dinner, take me somewhere. You often hear about a guy doing that, but when a girl does that, it's attractive!

—JUSTIN TIMBERLAKE, MUSICIAN IN BAND 'NSYNC

True Story
Beautiful Music

When I was in eighth grade, a ninth-grade boy played guitar and sang "Stairway to Heaven" at our school's talent show. The sound of his voice captivated me. That's all it took. I didn't even know what he looked like because I'd sat in the back of the auditorium.

I was determined to meet him, so I asked my friends if they knew his name. One of them did. I looked him up in the phone book and, with my heart pounding, called the number. His mom answered and went to get him. What would I say? I panicked for a moment. He picked up the phone. I told him I loved his singing, that he was great and truly talented. I asked if he would have lunch with me the next day. He said, "Sure."

We became good friends and soon fell in love. Am I ever glad I mustered the courage to reach out to him.

Sometimes instead of waiting for love to come to you, you can help it along. In my case that made all the difference!

— ELIZABETH CARLASSARE, WRITER

Quick List: Hot Dates

Sometimes what you do can be as fun as who goes with you. A well-planned date means a rewarding experience, even if the guy turns out to be a dud. Dinner, movies, and coffee are a start, but consider these ideas, too:

• Bowling
• A beach cleanup
• Mini golf
• Stargazing
• A ride on a tandem bike
• A picnic in the backyard

- A flea market
- An art museum or exhibit
- A bookstore event
- A hike
- A play or musical
- Paddleboating

FASCINATING FACT

When asked whether it's okay for a girl to call a boy and ask him out, seventy percent of the people in a recent Gallup poll said yes. When the same question was asked in 1950, only twenty-nine percent said yes.

Chapter 10

True Romance

 A hottie with a dozen long-stemmed roses on Valentine's Day. A fancy dinner. Gourmet chocolates with a lovey-dovey card. These are not unique ways to express affection, but they do score points.

And they're just the beginning when it comes to romance. About seventy-five percent of the people in a Wirthlin Worldwide survey agreed that "romance is just thoughtfulness." So basically any activity, gift, or gesture intended to strengthen love is romantic: holding hands, taking his pooch for a walk, sending a silly postcard, even doing boring chores.

Love is the cake and romance is the frosting. But cake is pretty bland without frosting. Romance is not a frivolous extra to be used in February, it's an everyday part of love.

Cool Quotes

Love is not satisfied by its mere existence. You still have to know how to express it. Preferably with verve, style, and humor.

—MONIQUE PIVOT, WRITER

[True romance] is to grown-ups what the entire inventory of a toy store is to children.

—MARIANNE WILLIAMSON, SPIRITUAL GURU

Romance is the glamour which turns the dust of everyday life into a golden haze.

—ELINOR GLYN, WRITER, ACTOR,
PRODUCER, DIRECTOR, 1864–1943

Romance is basically illusion and fantasy, excitement and newness. If it existed day in and day out in one long unbroken continuum, it would no longer be romance.

—EILEEN SILVA KINDIG, WRITER

Romance could be . . . seeing through someone else's eyes, feeling with their nerve endings, absorbing another culture or way of life from the inside, stretching our boundaries, and bringing into ourselves a wider view of the world.

—GLORIA STEINEM, WOMEN'S RIGHTS ACTIVIST, WRITER

You give me thoughtful gifts. . . . But the best thing is when I surprise you deep at work or you spot me in a crowd and your eyes light up with pleasure.

—HELEN EXLEY, EDITOR, PUBLISHER

Homely services rendered for love's sake have in them a poetry that is immortal.

—HARRIET BEECHER STOWE, WRITER, 1811–1896

Why is it that the most unoriginal thing we can say to one another is still the thing we long to hear? "I love you" is always a quotation.

— JEANETTE WINTERSON, WRITER

Guy's-Eye View

I'm a big believer in surprises. You've got to be romantic all the time.

— FREDDIE PRINZE, JR., ACTOR

The most romantic things a guy can do for a woman is be true, comfort her, and always listen.

— BILL BARNETT, 16

True Story
The Book of Love

One day, my boyfriend, Josh, gave me a gift—a hand-made book called *The Story of Michelle and Josh*. This children's-style book consisted of pictures of the two of us from birth, in childhood, in couplehood, and on trips we'd taken. The writing was heartwarming and awesome.

My eyes were puddles, and I could barely see to read the last two pages—the most beautiful pages I have ever and will ever read. The second-to-last page said, "So they decided they should always be together, forever. . . ." The last page read, "And here is a promise of forever." On the bottom right-hand corner of the page he had cut out a perfect square in the remaining twenty pages or so, where an engagement ring fit perfectly—as if it were in a box! After regaining my composure and wiping away my tears, of course I said yes.

It was truly the most beautiful day in our relationship, and we've shared some good ones. Here's to hopelessly romantic men!

—MICHELLE GHILOTTI MANDEL, EVENT DESIGNER

Love Poem

12 A.M.

I sat up, an idea in my head.
I blindly searched for the light switch.
Slipped on my glasses,
picked up a piece of paper,
grabbed my box of lipstick,
and placed myself on the floor.

I picked a bright red to write "I LOVE YOU."
Then placed different colors on my lips,
to be pressed against the paper.
Then climbed back into bed.

The next day,
after giving him the lipstick-covered paper,
I asked someone what could possess me to do this.

She smiled.
"You're in love."

I smiled.
"Yes, I am."

— ANDI CHRISMAN, 16

Quick List: Romantic Encounters

When asked what her most romantic experience was,
actor Lara Flynn Boyle said, "Being danced into a pool

fully clothed." Creativity adds spice to love. However, you can always fall back on these basics, which rated highest in a survey of what's romantic conducted at Bowling Green State University:

• Taking a walk
• Giving or receiving flowers
• Sharing a kiss
• Having a candlelight dinner
• Cuddling

FASCINATING FACTS

How did we get the expression "to wear your heart on your sleeve"? In the Middle Ages, young people drew names from a bowl to see who their valentines would be, and then wore the names on their sleeves for a week.

If you want to whisper sweet nothings in your love's ear, use the left ear. It's controlled by the right side of the brain—the side that processes emotions.

Want to send a special valentine? Put a prestamped, addressed valentine in a bigger first-class envelope and mail it (to arrive by February 3) to: Postmaster, Attn: Valentines, USPS, Loveland, CO 80538-9998. It will be hand-stamped with a historic valentine image and sent on to the person you've specified. For more information, see www.loveland.org/valentine/index.htm.

Chapter 11

Friends Forever?

"I just want to be friends."

Guys use these six disappointing little words all the time to back out of romantic or potentially romantic situations. It sounds at least somewhat encouraging; your friendship is still desired. But if you love someone, being solely friends will never be satisfying in the same way as being friends *and* in love.

"Just friends" does, however, take the pressure off, allowing you two to relax around each other and actually even *be* friends. That could lead to love (but don't hold your breath on this).

Don't give up on your buddies—both the ones who've laid the "just friends" line on you and the ones you've delegated to the pal pile.

Cool Quotes

It's like all of a sudden you look at this person who knows you, who you feel safe with, and you say, "Wow. Wait a minute . . . here he is."

—LAURA DERN, ACTOR

Perhaps, after all, romance did not come into one's life with pomp and blare. . . . Perhaps it crept to one's side like an old friend through quiet ways.

—L. M. MONTGOMERY, WRITER, 1874–1942

Any number of men are not only not classically handsome, they . . . are so smart and so funny and so charming and they pay so much attention to us that we think they are the most attractive men who ever lived.

—JILL CONNER BROWNE, PERFORMANCE ARTIST

One day you look at the person and you see something more than you did the night before. Like a switch has been flicked somewhere. And the person who was just a friend is . . . suddenly the only person you can ever imagine yourself with.

—DANA SCULLY, T.V. SHOW CHARACTER PLAYED BY GILLIAN ANDERSON

As you get older you realize an amazing friendship is great to establish. It doesn't matter if he's going to kiss you or not—that's only a consequence.

—DIANE VON FURSTENBERG, FASHION DESIGNER

We became friends, and then one day the shameless rascal declared his love for me. He said, "Give me a chance, and I will be your slave." And surely, I gave him that chance but he hasn't been my slave—he's been my life companion.

—CELIA CRUZ, SINGER

All love that has not friendship for its base,
Is like a mansion built upon the sand.
                    —ELLA WHEELER WILCOX, WRITER, 1850–1919

Guy's-Eye View

Came but for friendship, and took away love.
                    —THOMAS MOORE, POET, 1779–1852

True Stories
No Interest? No Problem

Golden hair, glacier-blue eyes, smooth lips, and a smile
that melted my heart. After spending four days with a
guy on a school trip, I'd fallen hard. On my way off the
bus I handed him a note with my number and asked
for his.

He didn't call, so I called him. We talked for an hour, and I felt that we clicked. He made me laugh and let me be myself. His attention made me feel special and like I was on top of the world. I was infatuated. I was in love. I used all the flirtatious weapons I knew of, but to no avail. Still, we talked for hours on end, until our phones died. We talked until the sun came up, until we got grounded. I wrote him notes I wouldn't give him, and I changed my routes to class so I could wave at him in the hallway.

What I didn't plan on was falling in friendship with him. In addition to having a crush on him, I loved him in a completely platonic way. Eventually, out of the awareness that I was afraid of someday losing his friendship, I realized a relationship might not be what I truly needed from him.

A few years and a million conversations later, he's still one of the most important people in my life. I've never kissed him, I've never been on a date with him, and I've never been able to call him my boyfriend, but I wouldn't have it any other way. I still tingle when he laughs and melt when he smiles, but I also have a friend who will last for the rest of my life, no matter how I love him.

—KRISTA QUESENBERRY, 17

Moment of Truth

When my boyfriend and I first met, we became good friends. We stayed close when he started to go out with one of my friends. They broke up after a few weeks, and he took it badly. When I comforted him and tried cheering him up, he told me I was the only one who cared.

Soon we were best friends, and we promised we'd stay that way. However, my feelings for him were growing. I didn't think he would feel the same way, and I didn't want to ruin our friendship, so I didn't say anything. But one day we were walking in the park, and he said, "I know we are really good friends, but do you want to take it further?"

Since then we have become much closer. When we're together I feel like a princess—not because he spends loads of money on me, but because I know he loves me so much.

—LYNDSAY RAWLE, 16

FASCINATING FACT

According to the book *Falling in Love* by Ayala Malach Pines, an estimated eighty-nine percent of relationships begin through people's repeated exposure to each other.

Chapter 12

Signed, Sealed, Delivered

Cell phones, e-mail, pagers, instant messages. Who could ask for easier ways to talk to the one you love?

The trouble is, the intensity gets lost with these everyday connection modes. They're great for "Hey" and "Love you," but only that old-fashioned, practically dead form of communication, the love letter, can pull a person's heartstrings the way you might like. Anything written by hand packs a bigger punch. And according to love-letter expert Antonia Fraser, writing is powerful because "letters can be carried around as talismans to refresh the memory," while phone calls can only be remembered.

Like anything else worth doing, writing a love letter takes some effort. But it's a small price to pay to bowl over your beloved.

Cool Quotes

The first glance to see how many pages there are, the second to see how it ends, the breathless first reading, the slow lingering over each phrase and each word, the taking possession, the absorbing of them, one by one, and finally the choosing of the one that will be carried in one's thoughts all day.

— EDITH WHARTON, WRITER, 1862–1937

Letters are above all useful as a means of expressing the ideal self; and no other method of communication is quite so good for this purpose.

— ELIZABETH HARDWICK, WRITER

I never realized before that a letter—a mere sheet of paper—could be such a spiritual thing—could emanate so much feeling.

—Tina Modotti, photographer, 1896–1942

To write a letter is to be alone with my thoughts in the conjured presence of another person.

—Vivian Gornick, sociologist, writer

Guy's-Eye View

Darling . . . I love you so much, much, much that it just hurts every minute I'm without you—do write every day because I love your letters so.

—F. Scott Fitzgerald, writer, 1896–1940,
in a letter to his wife, Zelda

I want to let her know how special she is. . . . Writing [love] letters is the most honest I can be.

—FREDDIE PRINZE, JR., ACTOR

True Stories
Attic Treasures

I always knew my grandparents loved each other. I saw it in the simple things they did, like holding hands in the car, sneaking a kiss when they thought no one was watching, and knowing exactly what to order for each other at a restaurant. But it wasn't until my sixteenth birthday that I realized the true depth of their love. That was when I found a pile of love letters from my grandfather nestled in the bottom of my grandma's old trunk. I read the delicate pages, which had yellowed with time, slowly savoring every word. My grandfather's words of love danced across the paper, and my heart stood still.

I took the letters to my grandmother, whose face lit up when she saw them. She called my grandfather into the kitchen and began reading them out loud. As she finished, my grandfather put his arms around her and said, "You know, hun, after forty-seven years, those words are still true."

In that moment I knew, without a doubt, that true love wasn't just something on the silver screen. It was real, and it lasted forever.

—SANDRA JACKSON, STUDENT

Express Mail

The first love letter Ian sent me said "Just because." It didn't need to say anything else. After that we started writing letters all the time, even though we only lived a subway ride apart. Our letters said things we couldn't say aloud and expressed a romantic poetry that would have been awkward in person. Each time I recognized the telltale watermark of his envelopes in my mailbox, I felt my heart swell.

Moving in together didn't stop us from writing letters. It was romantic and fun, and, yes, a little silly, but that's how love is. Sometimes we'd just send a postcard; other times a request for a date—anything to give that surge of elation we felt by knowing someone cared about us.

I define love by the most romantic love letter Ian ever sent me. The sentiment still stays in my mind:

"A funny thing happened to me the other day. I was walking down the avenue in the bitter cold, trying to get my errands done, and I realized I was smiling. Not just your average smile, but a big, goofy grin—the type reserved for drooling idiots and this fool in love. People gave me funny looks but I didn't care, I just kept smiling. Thank you for making me smile for no reason on a bitter cold day on Sixth Avenue."

—ROSALIE RUNG, ADVENTURER

Quick List: Letter-Writing Tips

Want to write a mushy letter to your sweetie? Here's how:

Go to the library or online and read love letters penned through the ages. The language may be outdated, but the sentiments are timeless.

- Turn on some classical or other romantic music
- Pull out a photo of your sweetie to get your emotions flowing
- Use nice stationery and a calligraphy pen or colored pens
- Write the letter by hand (even if you draft it on the computer)
- Use flowery phrases and get sentimental
- Wait a day and edit your first draft
- Close with a romantic phrase like "Forever yours"
- Stick on a love-themed stamp and a kiss mark

Chapter 13

The Right Knight

If you're like many girls, you have Mr. Right in your mind, but not in your life. When will he come along?

Part of the mystique of Mr. Right is that he hasn't arrived yet. He may indeed show up—either days or years from now. However, he might also not be what you imagine; in fact, you might not even recognize him. Relationship expert Susan Page says that of every one hundred happily married people, ninety-eight say their Mr. Right—the person they end up marrying arrives in a physical package they don't expect.

That's a good thing, because it implies that you've got a good chance of actually *finding* Mr. Right.

Cool Quotes

No matter how lovesick a woman is, she shouldn't take the first pill that comes along.

— JOYCE BROTHERS, PSYCHOLOGIST

Let us wait patiently for our counterparts. Even waiting in vain is better than willy-nilly marriage.

— ZHANG JIE, WRITER

I've discovered that the universe doesn't make it difficult for people to meet each other. It makes it pretty easy.

— DREW BARRYMORE, ACTOR

There is this feeling of great desperation to find the appropriate mate, but my experience really is that the older and more comfortable you get with yourself, the easier it is to find somebody.

—NINA TOTENBERG, RADIO CORRESPONDENT

My parents say, "True love happens when you are not looking. . . . And when you fall in love from that place, that's the best kind."

—CHRISTIE BRINKLEY, MODEL

I always tell people looking for love to wait for that "I won the lottery" feeling—wait, wait, wait! Don't read articles about how to trap, seduce or hypnotize a mate. Don't worry about your lipstick or your height, because it's not going to matter.

—LOIS SMITH BRADY, WRITER

If the right man does not come along, there are many fates far worse. One is to have the wrong man come along.

—LETITIA BALDRIGE, ETIQUETTE EXPERT

Guy's-Eye View

At the end of the day, there's nothing more important than finding the person you want to be with for the rest of your life.

—EDDIE BURNS, ACTOR, FILMMAKER

True Stories
A Good Deal at the Mall

I'd always pictured my perfect man as someone tall with dark hair, eyes, and skin. Someone successful in his career, quiet and serious, and without children but heading toward marriage and family. So when I started a job at a mall store, I didn't consider dating the guy who worked at the kiosk across from me. He was light skinned with brown-blonde hair and obviously not in a serious career. He already had a child and couldn't care less about getting married.

One night he struck up a conversation and asked me out. I decided to risk it. Eight months have gone by since that night, and although we've broken up, this relationship has been a great learning experience for me. It has taught me that sometimes "perfect" isn't what we dream it to be. The best things in life may be right in front of our faces, but we don't see them because we're too busy looking for something "better."

Step out and take the risk—it may be the best decision you ever make.

—MELISSA SISLER, RETAIL SALESPERSON

The Love Monster

He wasn't my type—he was dark and I preferred blonds—but his tenacity and charm slowly melted my resolve and I became flattered, then interested.

We had been dating for a few weeks when he proposed a weekend in the French countryside with two other couples. The six of us drove into a quaint little village to get supplies at a small grocery store. The three Frenchmen, considering themselves quite gourmet, decided to go into the shop themselves to pick out fresh produce and meat, leaving the three women outside at our leisure. Being American, I wasn't sure whether to find this arrogant or generous. But then my man took my hand and together we skipped inside: I became the only woman invited into this exclusive culinary club. He swung me around behind him, pulling my arms around his waist, and began filling them up with merchandise: eggs, a bottle of Coke, a head of lettuce, a box of cookies—he piled my arms higher and higher. We were like a four-armed monster, giggling at first, then shaking with laughter as we precariously made our way up and down the aisles. At one point I looked around and saw the townspeople staring at us in consternation, the women not without envy.

I suddenly realized that he had won my heart. I wanted my life to be filled with moments like this. And I've become much more open-minded about hair color.

—COURTNEY JONES, STUDENT

Love Poems

. . . And Then the Prince Knelt Down and Tried to Put the Glass Slipper on Cinderella's Foot

I really didn't notice that he had a funny nose.

And he certainly looked better all dressed up in fancy clothes.

He's not nearly as attractive as he seemed the other night.

So I think I'll pretend that this glass slipper feels too tight.

—JUDITH VIORST, POET, FROM *IF I WERE IN CHARGE OF THE WORLD AND OTHER WORRIES*

FASCINATING FACTS

Good news for shiny, happy people: According to researchers Clark and Watson, you're more likely to meet someone special when you're in a good mood and having fun.

In a poll for *Time* and CNN, almost eighty percent of those surveyed thought they'd eventually find the perfect mate.

Chapter 14

Tough Love

 Sometimes, despite your best efforts, love lets you down. You never get to date (or even talk to) your crush. Or maybe you do, but for some reason, the chemistry fizzles. Or things go great, right up until he suddenly says good-bye.

"It is better to have loved and lost than never to have loved at all" is small consolation, but there's some truth to it. If a dating situation ultimately proves not right for either of you, you're still a wiser, more well-rounded person for every emotion you've invested in it.

So whether you're ready to leave a relationship or you can't get one started, don't despair. The love of your life could be waiting in the wings. When the time is right, the show will start.

Cool Quotes

Love is a fire. But whether it is going to warm your heart or burn down your house, you can never tell.

—JOAN CRAWFORD, ACTOR, 1908–1977

I don't have any regrets, because I learned so much from him about love and about myself, and that's beautiful.

—ALYSSA MILANO, ACTOR

Bad guys, like root vegetables, are good for us and help us grow.

—BROOK HERSEY, WRITER

Love hurts and it makes you smile, it stings like a bee, and yet it is your cure.

—MARIANNA RYBAK, COLLEGE STUDENT

A woman has got to love a bad man once or twice in her life, to be thankful for a good one.

—MARJORIE KINNAN RAWLINGS, WRITER, 1896–1953

I've had my share of love woes. . . . They haven't all been great experiences, but they have all been useful because they've helped me to figure out what I do and don't like in men.

—TYRA BANKS, MODEL

True Story
A Lesson in Love

I loved Steven McDonald from afar for months, though we never formally met. And then something amazing happened. I was taking driver's ed, and so was he . . . and we were in the same car. I totally freaked out. I worried about my clothes. I decided to wear perfume since we would be so close.

The next week, when I got in the car, my heart beat like a cymbal. I was sure everybody could hear it.

Steven was the first to drive. After a few blocks, I saw a small child riding his tricycle on the side of the road, all alone. Suddenly he toppled over. He lay there crying, his mouth bleeding.

"Stop!" I shouted to Steven.

"Why?" asked Mr. Barrett, the driving instructor. He had not seen the kid.

"A kid just got hurt, and he's all alone."

"Turn around," said Mr. Barrett to Steven.

"He doesn't need us," said Steven. "He'll be fine." And he kept driving.

Mr. Barrett finally made Steven turn around. By that time the boy's mother was there, comforting him.

When Steven took his place in the back seat next to me, I didn't care how he looked. He had lost his charm. And I realized I had never really loved him; I had loved only the idea of him, the idea of love. I had made him up.

—CAMRYN GREEN, WRITER, HUMORIST, COMMENTATOR; FROM WHOLEFAMILY.COM

Love Poems

I'd Love You If Only

Your voice, soft and deep,
Rings in my ears,
Words soft, sweet, and smooth as taffy
Full of praise for someone else.
I'd love you if only
You didn't belong to another.

Your eyes, a piece of the gorgeous night sky,
Look straight into mine,
warm, and full of love
For that other girl.
I'd love you if only
You weren't somebody else's.

Your heart, pure and true,
I want to be mine,
But it beats for my friend.

—HELENE MARIE ROSE, 13

I waited
For the phone to ring
And when at last
It didn't
I knew it was you.

—ELEANOR BRON, COMIC ACTOR

Chapter 15

Bye, Bye Love

 You've broken up. You feel horrible, and you keep remembering the special moments and aspects of the relationship that you hate to lose. And then there's that nagging thought, "If only I could have done (fill in the blank) differently, maybe we'd still be together."

The pain of breaking up can seem unbearable. Just know that once you can move through (not around) these feelings, your emotional state will improve a little every day. Don't worry, it *will* improve. If you want proof, think of all the people—such as celebrities, with their highly publicized breakups—who parted ways but picked themselves up and went on to love again, even more passionately.

If they can do it, so can you.

Cool Quotes

I feel strong as a horse and so fragile I could lose it at any moment.

—HELEN HUNT, ACTOR, ON
SPLITTING UP WITH HER HUSBAND

Only time can heal your broken heart, just as only time can heal his broken arms and legs.

—MISS PIGGY, MUPPET

Nobody wants to be someone who broke someone else's heart.

—JENNIFER LOVE HEWITT, ACTOR

A breakup is a good experience for learning what to do and what *not* to do next time.

—JESSICA RITACCO, 15

The time you spend grieving over a man should never exceed the amount of time you actually spent with him.

—RITA RUDNER, COMEDIAN

Guy's-Eye View

From each of these men, and from yourself too, you will draw some lesson that will help you cope better with your next love—which will, you'll see, again be the "only" one and "for ever," like the one before.

—JORGE ENRIQUE ADOUM, WRITER,
IN A LETTER TO A LOVELORN GIRL

Love is the ultimate parachute jump. We could get hurt, we could get rejected. However, the greater risk is we never see our tender, emotional, vulnerable self.

—JOHN AMODEO, WRITER

True Stories
Heart of Darkness

I had the biggest crush on Matt, so I was amazed when a friend told me he was going to ask me out. But that night, another friend told me not to say yes if he did. I wish I had asked why.

The next day he asked me out. I said yes, and it was the best day of my life. But the day after that, he told me he felt uncomfortable with the relationship and that it would be best if we were just friends, and, oh, by the way, he liked another girl.

I felt like jumping off a cliff. One day, and I was already getting dumped. I heard later that it was a dare for him to ask me out and that he just felt sorry for me. I wish I had been prepared for what happened, but I wasn't, and I'm not sure how I could have been. And unfortunately I still adore him, and it seems I always will.

— JESSICA BETTENCOURT, 13

Light at the End of the Tunnel

Walking away from a two-and-a-half year relationship was the hardest thing I've ever done. It took me almost eight months to even acknowledge the reality of the situation. I had tunnel vision and was allowing myself to see only the thin sliver of happiness the relationship held. It was a relationship of emotional abuse, nonstop fighting, and obsession. My ex-boyfriend was controlling and insisted that I have no friends—boys or girls. I spent many nights crying myself to sleep and waiting for his attention and comfort. I was constantly irritable and short-tempered with everyone, even my sweet little dog.

After being out of the relationship now for a while, I'm back to the happy, warm, energetic, and patient person I used to be. While it was the hardest thing to walk away, I'm a better and stronger person for it. Now I know that no emotional obstacle is too big for me.

—SARAH MAURICE, STUDENT

Love Poem

Closing Doors

You opened your door
and ushered me in,
tempting me with visions of
what might have been.

When I finally realized
I was in the wrong place,
I stepped outside and
closed the door in your face.

The sound the door made
could barely be heard,
but that doesn't matter
'cause my heart said the word . . .

Good-bye.
— ALANNA WEBB, CHEMICAL ENGINEER, WEB ENTREPRENEUR

Romantic Lyrics

I've got all my life to live,
I've got all my love to give and I'll survive.
— GLORIA GAYNOR, SINGER-
SONGWRITER, FROM "I WILL SURVIVE"

In a study by Michael Liebowitz of the New York State Psychiatric Institute, when people accustomed to falling in and out of love went through breakups, they ate lots of chocolate. There's a scientific excuse: chocolate contains phenylethylamine, which is associated with that giddy, nervous sensation of being in love.

Chapter 16

Party of One

 For every married couple in the United States, there are 1.5 single adults. This means you stand a chance of being on your own at some point.

If you find yourself unattached—now or in the future—you might like it. A growing number of women are choosing to stay single. One reason is that in these modern times, couples don't depend on each other for survival, as the hunters and gatherers did years ago.

Being on your own is also good preparation for being attached, because if you can make it solo, you can make it as a self-sufficient half of a duo. The independence and perspective you acquire alone will make your time together all the better.

Cool Quotes

A woman without a man is like a fish without a bicycle.

—Gloria Steinem, women's rights activist, writer

I believe we all have one true love, but for now I prefer not to know where mine is.

—Brittany Murphy, actor

There could be a man around the next corner who says, "I love this house, all your nutty friends and that you're gone for two weeks at a time." . . . But if he doesn't come along, I'm very happy being single.

—Stevie Nicks, singer-songwriter

Everything comes in waves. And you've gotta believe that you'll get another good wave, but it's also good to just sit on the surfboard and enjoy the sun.

—Charlize Theron, actor

I enjoy the flow of my own energy. . . . Right now I'm sort of dating myself.

—DIANE LANE, ACTOR

When you are single, it is tempting to gaze at couples longingly and wonder, "Why not me?" When you are part of a couple, sometimes you look at single people and wonder, "When can I do that again?"

—SARK, ARTIST, WRITER

I am not living with anyone; I am not engaged to anyone. I am, therefore, single. And I'm loving it.

—LARA FLYNN BOYLE, ACTOR

I'm not giving up on [men], but . . . I can be alone and be happy. With books and music . . . I don't get lonely. I'm my own hobby, honey.

—WHOOPI GOLDBERG, ACTOR

True Story
Better Shop Around

Jim and I were high school sweethearts who thought we'd get married after college. Then we had a misunderstanding, and I called the whole relationship off. But I wasn't sure if I was doing the right thing. Was I giving up the one man who wanted to be with me for the rest of my life? Would I ever find anyone else?

After we broke up I decided to clear my head and figure out what type of guy I really wanted. I spent a couple of years on my own, in the process discovering that I could be happy without a man. That was a lesson my mother had taught me, but I'd forgotten it along the way.

Then Randy came into my life. We've been together for three years. I'm so glad I didn't settle for the first person who came along. I shopped around and got exactly what I wanted.

— JESSICA LITWIN, RECEPTIONIST

Quick List: A Life of One's Own

Here are some benefits that girls cite in being single:

• Being able to flirt with whomever you want
• You can come and go on your own schedule
• Guy friends: as many as you can fit in that schedule
• More time for girls' night out
• No need to watch football or action movies
• One word: freedom

FASCINATING FACT

Eighty-one percent of girls in a recent *YM* poll said they could lead a perfectly happy life without getting married.

Chapter 17

A Little Respect

 Have you ever felt like you weren't good enough for a guy?

"You can be in a situation and fall in love and just give yourself away, and then you find yourself in this pattern where you can't get out," says actor Jennifer Lopez.

To avoid that pattern, you need to keep your self-respect. When you value yourself, you attract guys who psychologically "match" your high level of respect. If you send signals that you can be taken advantage of or abused in any way, this is a slippery slope that could put you in danger.

If your relationship destination doesn't feel right, turn around. There's a better road ahead!

Cool Quotes

It's not about how much you love someone, it's about who you are when you're with them.

—DIANE FARR, TV SHOW HOST, ACTOR

When you love yourself first, you're strong enough to be honest with the person you love.

—ANGIE GAGE, 16

When a girl is strong inside . . . her biggest problem becomes which guy she should choose from all the cool guys who are interested in her.

—GILDA CARLE, PSYCHOLOGIST

Just "finding a guy" was not what I needed. From now on, I will only spend time with a man who treats me like gold!

—MICHELLE THOMAS, SPORTS MARKETING PROFESSIONAL

Don't throw away your dreams on a relationship that is detrimental to your future. You have to seek out your potential, and relationships aren't the end-all, be-all.

—REESE WITHERSPOON, ACTOR

I do feel happier [with a man], but when I look to the relationship to make me feel complete, I'm on insecure ground.

—BROOKE SHIELDS, ACTOR

A lot of girls believe they have to look like actors and models and that they have to be superthin in order to be considered beautiful and to find a boyfriend. Well, I've never had a problem with guys. I think it's because I accept myself.

—MIA TYLER, PLUS-SIZE MODEL

We may all be on the lookout for a man, but we want the right man on our terms. We are not about to compromise!

—BEYONCE KNOWLES, SINGER-SONGWRITER

Guy's-Eye View

Immature love says, I love you because I need you. Mature love says, I need you because I love you.

—ERICH FROMM, SOCIOLOGIST, PHILOSOPHER, 1900–1980

True Story
Give Me a Break!

When I was a girl, I had very low self-confidence and didn't think boys would be interested in me. So when one came along, I desperately grabbed him and never considered looking at others. I always assumed that the relationship I was in would last forever. And I never took time between relationships to explore who I was and what kind of life would make me happy.

So I decided to take a break. I spent three years exploring spirituality and creativity and making female friends. With a new sense of balance in my life, I felt I'd have a better chance of recognizing a compatible mate if one were to show up. Lo and behold, one did. And thanks to what I'd learned about myself, I recognized him!

—BONNIE SANDLER, ARTIST

Quick List: How Does Your Relationship Rate?

Answer these questions to assess whether your romance is working.

1. Do close friends tell you your relationship is not good for you?

   Yes   No

2. Do you create reasons for staying in the relationship that, when you look at them objectively, don't balance out the negative aspects of the relationship?

   Yes   No

3. Do you feel dread or terror when you consider ending the relationship?

    Yes   No

4. When you try to end the relationship, do you feel physical withdrawal symptoms that go away when you're together again?

    Yes   No

5. When you've ended the relationship, do you feel completely alone and lost in the world?

    Yes   No

If you answered yes to any of these questions, take a closer look at your situation. Ask someone you trust to help you determine the best next steps.

—ADAPTED FROM *CRACKING THE LOVE CODE* BY JANET O'NEAL

Need guidance on getting out of a troubling relationship? Check out the resources on page 168.

FASCINATING FACT

In a study by O'Keefe and Trester summarized in the journal *Violence Against Women*, of more than 1,000 high school students, forty-five percent of girls and forty-three percent of boys said they'd experienced dating violence at least once.

Chapter 18

It Takes Two

 When you fall in love, you may feel like figuratively melding yourself into your sweetheart to form one being. To a certain degree, love partners do merge their identities and influence each other's thoughts, feelings, and behavior. Couples can even grow to *look like* one another over the years.

However, there's a limit to this "two-become-one" business. If you and your beau were trees, would you want to share the same trunk? It would be confining, to say the least.

Romantic relationships need space in order for each partner to thrive. Instead of blowing out your individual candles and forming one flame, picture all three flames. This should keep the fire of your connection burning bright.

Cool Quotes

The only kind of relationships that work, and work forever, are the kind between two complete, independent people.

— FIONA APPLE, SINGER-SONGWRITER

Love is like quicksilver in the hand.
Leave the fingers open and it stays.
Clutch it, and it darts away.

— DOROTHY PARKER, HUMORIST, WRITER, 1893–1967

Whenever one tries too desperately to be physically close to some beloved person, whenever one throws all one's longing for that person, one is really giving him short change. For one has no reserves left then for a true encounter.

— ETTIE HILLESUM, DIARIST, 1914–1943

You should be walking alongside your partner, not jumping piggyback on them.

—Christina Applegate, actor

Ideally, both members of a couple in love free each other to new and different worlds.

—Anne Morrow Lindbergh, writer

The capacity to love is tied to being able to . . . be with someone else in a manner that is not about your desire to possess them, but to be with them.

—bell hooks, writer

I thought I could be completed by a man, but I now know I can be a complete woman and find a complete man.

—Cathy Jones, comic actor

Guy's-Eye View

Let there be spaces in your togetherness/ . . . For the pillars of the temple stand apart/And the oak tree and the cypress grow not in each other's shadow.

—KAHLIL GIBRAN, WRITER, 1883–1931

Some of us think holding on makes us strong; but sometimes it is letting go.

—HERMANN HESSE, WRITER, 1877–1962

True Story
Not in the Cards

My ex-boyfriend, Dan, and I dated for six years. Dan was smart, kind, loving, funny, my best friend—everything I'd always wanted. My family and friends adored him and told me I was lucky to have such a terrific guy. But the more serious we got, the more I doubted we were meant to be together. Something told me he wasn't The One, yet I couldn't break it off. I'd invested so much in our relationship, and I didn't want to hurt him.

I finally realized I was just afraid to be alone. I had to follow my own path, even if it meant never finding someone else. So I broke it off. At first it was really tough. My friend sent me homemade "feel better" cards to cheer me up. Her kind notes inspired me to launch my own greeting-card company, something I never would've had the courage to do if I'd stayed with Dan.

So much has changed since then. My business has taken off, and that has given me more confidence. There's no one special in my life yet, but I've met a lot of fun and interesting people. Leaving Dan was one of the most painful decisions I've made, but in the end everything turned out all right.

—MARIA PEEVEY, ENTREPRENEUR

Love Poem

I Am

I am a carousel
up, down, up
round and round
where I end
and you begin I wonder
I've lost the me
somewhere along the way.
Stop.
I want to get off.
First I must be me, only then
will there again be an us.
But for now,
just for now,
I am a carousel.

—CJ HECK, WRITER

Chapter 19

Friendly Advice

 You're spending practically every minute with your boyfriend. Say, when was the last time you saw your other friends?

That's right, you have other people in your life, and they're not amused. Take a breather from your honey now and then and demonstrate that they're still important.

By the way, they're important to your romance, too. You can bounce your relationship issues off of them. Plus, the time you spend with your friends will make your life feel more balanced. And of course, it pays to keep the communication going with your friends so that if the romance doesn't work out, you can go running into their arms. It works best if those arms are open.

Cool Quotes

Friendship is too important to be cast aside. And sometimes, it even lasts longer than Love of My Life Number Thirty-two.

—JANN MITCHELL, WRITER

I adore men, but women friends are what hold your life together.

—NANCY COLLINS, TV CORRESPONDENT

Though Love be deeper, Friendship is more wide.

—CORINNE ROOSEVELT ROBINSON, SISTER OF
PRESIDENT THEODORE ROOSEVELT, 1861–1933

To throw over a friend for some snacky *dude du jour* is, well, short-sighted.

—MINDY MORGENSTERN, WRITER

Men are the spice. . . . Women are the meat and potatoes.

—PATRICIA MATSON, BUSINESSWOMAN

No matter who broke your heart or how long it takes to heal, you'll never get through it without your friends.
—CARRIE BRADSHAW, T.V. CHARACTER
PLAYED BY ACTOR SARAH JESSICA PARKER

I learned about the power of first love from the boy at school and about the staying power of friendship from the girl across the street.

—AISHA D. GAYLE, COLLEGE STUDENT

Men are like buses . . . you sit at the stop long enough and another one comes along—but girlfriends are like Maseratis . . . few and far between.

—DIANE FARR, TV SHOW HOST, ACTOR

Guy's-Eye View

Friendship is precious, not only in the shade, but in the sunshine of life, and thanks to a benevolent arrangement of things, the greater part of life is sunshine.

—THOMAS JEFFERSON, U.S. PRESIDENT, 1743–1826

True Story
Lost and Found

When my friend Lucy started dating her boyfriend, she got completely wrapped up in him. She even told me she wouldn't have much time for me anymore because he was the most important thing. While I appreciated her honesty, I felt sad and abandoned. I went on with my life and focused on other friends and interests.

One night the phone rang at 1 A.M. It was Lucy, crying

because her boyfriend had just dumped her. I thought it was ironic that she needed me only then, because she'd shifted all of her attention to him. But there was no doubt I wanted to be there for her in that moment. Girlfriends may at times let each other down, but they're also the ones who are there for us when we really need them.

— SARAH LONGAKER, NONPROFIT ORGANIZATION DIRECTOR

Chapter 20

Mate for Each Other

 In earlier generations, most people didn't go looking for their soulmate, or even imagine that one existed. People were so focused on the nitty-gritty of family and community life that they had very little time to worry about the quality of relationships. Now, whole books have been written about the pursuit of one's soulmate.

A soulmate is not necessarily someone perfect. Being with them might feel fated or like you've known each other before. Or you might have a series of things in common.

Whether you're destined to be lifelong partners, or, for some reason, you can only be friends, treasure these deep connections. Because that's what love is really about: two souls discovering common ground and walking it together.

Cool Quotes

I am like a falling star who has finally found her place next to another in a lovely constellation, where we will sparkle in the heavens forever.

—AMY TAN, WRITER

It doesn't matter what you do or where you live—there are no boundaries or barriers if two people are destined to be together.

—JULIA ROBERTS, ACTOR

'Twas not my lips you kissed, but my soul.

—JUDY GARLAND, SINGER, ACTOR, 1922–1969

We live through them as directly as through ourselves. . . . We push back our hair because theirs is in their eyes.

—NAN FAIRBROTHER, WRITER, 1913–1971

When you meet somebody you know you're supposed to be with, your potential as an individual becomes greater.

— KATE HUDSON, ACTOR

The house is just the shell. . . . Sting is my home.

— TRUDIE STYLER, ACTOR, ACTIVIST, WIFE OF STING

Guy's-Eye View

Love is composed of a single soul inhabiting two bodies.

— ARISTOTLE, PHILOSOPHER, 384–322 B.C.

True Story
Ahoy, (Room) Mate

When an old friend called to see if I would like to rent a house with him and his friend, I agreed. We met at a coffee shop and signed the lease. I didn't think too much about the other roommate, Chris, but a week later, after two hours of chatter, we were both taken by our similarities. As he would start to say something about relationships, life, or society, I would finish the thought in my head. On the way home I told myself I couldn't date him.

One night we went out with one of Chris's friends and his girlfriend. The girlfriend, after hearing us complain about our dating prospects, said we were obviously meant for each other. Later that night we admitted that we were interested in one another but were hesitant because of the living situation. So we decided to allow ourselves to feel the way we did but not act on it. Getting to know one another was the priority, and it was easy because we lived together—there was no hiding who we were.

At Christmas we finally became a couple. Neither of us has felt this comfortable with someone, and we make each other happier than we could ever have imagined. Whoever would have thought the decision to take a leap of faith and move in with my friend could lead me to the love of my life?

— JENNIFER SCHWARZ, SOFTWARE CONSULTANT

Love Poem

Soul Mate

His soul the midnight whistle
reaching through vast darkness
echoes the lament of my lonely spirit.
My reality lies in his arms, his vision,
and in the rhythm of his breath
as his heart beats out life
to love me.

— SUSAN FRIDKIN, WRITER

Romantic Lyrics

When my soul was in the lost-and-found
You came along to claim it.

—CAROLE KING, SINGER-SONGWRITER,
FROM "NATURAL WOMAN"

Chapter 21

Ever After

Just as a rosebud starts out perfect-looking and then unfolds to reveal many layers, the initial intensity and strong physical attraction of dating give way to a more mellow, multifaceted experience. When this happens, don't be alarmed. "Lots of people assume that if the energy lessens, something must be wrong," says Charlene Kamper, a high school teacher who designed a "Relationships 101" class. "They don't realize this is a natural pattern."

A committed relationship holds the fulfillment of knowing that your special someone wants a long-term connection. You have an opportunity to really trust, know, and understand each other, and to enjoy the feeling of comfort that this brings.

Love long and prosper.

Cool Quotes

I want you to know that I'll be with you for the long haul, no matter what. You're still you. And I love you.
—DANA REEVE, WIFE OF ACTOR CHRISTOPHER REEVE,
AFTER HE WAS PARALYZED IN AN ACCIDENT

Neither of us is deluded enough to think that every morning we'll wake up in love. We very well may, but if we don't, neither of us would panic.
—TÉA LEONI, ACTOR

For me, he's still the man I fell in love with in high school.
—TIPPER GORE, FORMER SECOND LADY

A relationship is going to evolve to a point where you're comfortable putting your hair up in a scrunchie so it looks like a water spout coming out of your head.

—LEAH REMINI, ACTOR

Habit, of which passion must be wary, may all the same be the sweetest part of love.

—ELIZABETH BOWEN, WRITER, 1899–1973

Guy's-Eye View

Grow old with me! The best is yet to be.

—ROBERT BROWNING, POET, 1812–1889

True Story
A Love for All Seasons

Every girl wonders how she will recognize love when it comes along. For me, it was the flutter in my heart when I first set eyes on him. And when he nodded at everything my mother said, that clinched it for me. As time passed, there were other signs: Placing a gentle hand on my back to guide me through a doorway, handing me a flower—just one—for no particular occasion, and, best of all, the smile on his face when I walked into the room.

These are small things, but they are gestures upon which love builds. True love does not diminish with the passing of time. Instead, it mellows and soothes and digs itself deeper into your heart.

—MONA TURA, WRITER

Love Poem

When

When fire's freezing cold,
when snow is boiling hot,
when birds forget to sing,
I'll still forget you not.
When every story ends,
when spring does not renew,
when all the clocks have stopped,
then I'll stop loving you.

—EVE MERRIAM, POET, 1916–1992,
FROM *VALENTINE'S DAY STORIES AND POEMS*

Romantic Lyrics

You are safe in my heart,
And my heart will go on and on.
—CELINE DION, SINGER-SONGWRITER, AS PERFORMED
IN THE LOVE THEME FROM *TITANIC*

FASCINATING FACT

Scientists say that on average, the highly romantic phase of a relationship, during which the partners can't get enough of each other, only lasts eighteen months to three years.

Chapter 22

Tying the Knot

 At some point with Mr. Right, the Big question may be asked: Will you take the guy to be your hubby?

Millions of American girls and women dream of floating down the aisle in a boofy white dress and proclaiming, "I do." Of course, the fact that weddings are such wonderful rituals and celebrations makes this an easy decision.

While some people don't view marriage as a requirement for lasting love, there are lots of advantages to not just *getting married* but *being* married and formally joining your life with someone else's. Some women see it as a way of deepening their commitment. Others like the stability. And there's always that part about "to have and to hold, from this day forward."

Cool Quotes

"Marry me!" Two words that change your life.

—WENDY GOLDBERG AND BETTY GOODWIN, WRITERS

[Marriage] doesn't necessarily have anything to do with the signing of the paper. It's just a way of bringing everybody together and celebrating our relationship.

—KATE HUDSON, ACTOR

We were looking for a way to say, "We love and want to be responsible for each other." . . . Thanks to all those who worked hard to transform [marriage] from a tradition of patriarchy and possession into a partnership.

—GLORIA STEINEM, WOMEN'S RIGHTS ACTIVIST, WRITER

Marriage isn't an *institution*. It's an *adventure*. . . . Having a fabulous life adventure with one other person.

—HELEN GURLEY BROWN, EDITOR, WRITER

We agreed when we got married that "failure isn't an option." This gave us freedom—to be who we truly are without worrying that the other person will leave when the going gets tough.

—JUDY HOCTOR, HOMEMAKER

Marriage is not a ritual or an end. It is a long, intricate, intimate dance together, and nothing matters more than your own sense of balance and your choice of partner.

—AMY BLOOM, WRITER

That quiet mutual gaze of a trusting husband and wife is like the first moment of rest or refuge from a great weariness or a great danger.

—GEORGE ELIOT (PEN NAME OF MARY ANN EVANS), WRITER, 1819–1880

Guy's-Eye View

My most brilliant achievement was my ability to persuade my wife to marry me.

—WINSTON CHURCHILL, PRIME MINISTER OF GREAT BRITAIN, 1874–1965

I was looking at her in the rearview mirror, and I thought, *I'm going to marry her.* And I turned to my friend who was sitting shotgun, and I told him, "Remember this day and two years from now I'll tell you what just went through my head." He just goes, "You don't have to tell me, I know."

—MATTHEW LILLARD, ACTOR

True Stories
Engagement Rink

My boyfriend Craig and I went ice skating at Wollman Rink in Central Park on the two-year anniversary of our first (blind) date. It was a clear and cold Saturday night, and there must have been three hundred skaters. After a few laps Craig asked me to do a spin, so we skated out to the center of the rink, which is kept clear for figure skaters. After a few spins I saw him kneeling down on one knee, and I thought he was going to lace up his skate. I skated over to tell him he wasn't supposed to do that on the ice. He pulled out a platinum diamond ring, sparkling brightly from the lights reflecting off the ice. He looked into my eyes and said, "Theresa, will you marry me?"

I was so shocked that I basically dove on him and started to cry. I held onto him as tightly as I could and said yes. Finally, as we stood up and Craig slipped the ring on my finger, we realized that nobody was skating. We were surrounded by three hundred people with the most amazed, happy looks on their faces. Craig yelled, "She said yes!" and the whole place erupted in cheers. We were mobbed like we had just won the World Series. We skated around a few more times like the king and queen of the prom. I felt like the most special person on earth.

—TERRI DALE, CLOTHING DESIGNER

Up on the Roof

When my friend Katy and I were thirteen, we climbed onto her parents' roof and carved our initials and those of the boys we liked in the shingles, encircling them with big, lopsided hearts. We thought this ritual would make B.S. and P.M. fall in love with us and eventually lead to a double marriage.

Fast-forward eighteen years. We married guys who just happened to be best friends. Their initials are different from the ones we carved years earlier, but I like to think that our teen ritual was what worked the magic. Or maybe some relationships are just meant to be.

—GRETCHEN DEAN, CLOWN

FASCINATING FACTS

In 1960, the average age at which American women got married was twenty; today it's twenty-five.

Why do people wear their wedding ring on the third finger of the left hand? A vein in this finger is said to go directly to the heart.

Chapter 23

Keeping It Together

 You've probably heard the odds: More than half of all marriages in the United States end in divorce. It seems that *staying* in love isn't as easy as *falling* in love.

While there's no magic ingredient that you can stir into your relationship to preserve it for eternity, there are certain things you can do to improve your chances of success. As anyone in a long-term relationship will tell you, it takes work. You've both got to be willing to talk through issues, iron out problems, and forgive.

The good news is that plenty of couples do stay together, many 'til death do they part. Somebody's got to be behind the winning half of the statistics. Why not you?

Cool Quotes

The best way to hold a man is in your arms.
— MAE WEST, ACTOR, 1892–1980

Knowing how to fight is a good thing. And humor is the greatest way of making the fight disappear.
— MARLO THOMAS, ACTOR, ACTIVIST

Do not take love for granted. As soon as you do, it will disappear.
— ZOE THRISCUTT, 16

Love doesn't just sit there, like a stone, it has to be made, like bread; remade all the time, made new.
— URSULA K. LE GUIN, WRITER

Love has nothing to do with what you are expecting to get—only with what you are expecting to give—which is everything.

—KATHARINE HEPBURN, ACTOR

Valuing the differences and being OK with not needing to agree with each other. That to me is how relationships don't start exploding.

—TORI AMOS, SINGER-SONGWRITER

Being honestly in love ... means being completely responsible for your fifty percent and not kidding yourself that it's really a seventy-thirty relationship and he's got waaaay more problems than you do.

—MINNIE DRIVER, ACTOR

Guy's-Eye View

You must treat each other like an egg: Hold it in your arms and don't let it crack.

— JAMES BROLIN, ACTOR

Romantic Lyrics

So if you want it to get stronger you'd better not let go. You've got to hold on longer if you want your love to grow.

— SADE, SINGER-SONGWRITER

Quick List: Staying Power

Here's what teens recommend for a strong relationship:

Don't flirt with my friends. And never ignore me when you're around your guy friends. Girls, especially me, *hate* that.

—JULIA JURKIEWICZ, 15

Know that I am not your property, and you aren't the center of my universe. I don't have to tell you where I'm going, who with . . . all that junk. I don't have to always be with you.

—ZOE VRABEL, 13

Be communicative. I like to know what people are thinking and why they do what they do. Be decisive. I am an easygoing guy who has fun doing anything. But I hate making all the decisions—I don't like one person relationships.

—JAMES M. BAKER, 17

Never cancel our plans so you can go out with your friends. Please don't take out your anger on me when you are fighting with your parents or friends.

—JUSTIN CARR, 16, FROM *PARADE* MAGAZINE

FASCINATING FACT

When married people were asked what characteristics of their relationships kept them happily together, these five were tops: Good communication, a sense of humor, and being able to resolve conflicts, adapt to change, and show affection.

Chapter 24

Crazy for You

He's got a smile that lights up the very depths of your being. Or he's a fantastic listener who knows how to keep a secret—and he shares his dreams with you. Maybe he's got a knack for making you bust up laughing, or he's a tender soul who's not afraid to cry with you.

Why do you love him? Or, as poet Elizabeth Barrett Browning put it, "How do I love thee? Let me count the ways."

Here's a sampling of why women and girls love men and boys—a tribute to all the good guys on the planet, whether they're in your arms right now or waiting patiently for you to discover them tomorrow.

Cool Quotes

He has such a great sense of humor. Sometimes, when we go to parties and he is sent to what we call "Spousal Siberia," he'll go up to people and introduce himself as Mr. Amy Tan.

—AMY TAN, WRITER, ON HUSBAND LOU

I love character lines, little wrinkles, little scars. I love eyes that you look into and find a dark, vast place of stories and knowledge.

—JENNIFER LOVE HEWITT, ACTOR

There's something about his spirit and his soul. . . . He's a gentleman.

—JENNIFER ANISTON, ACTOR, ON HUSBAND BRAD PITT

We're total opposites. He's a city slicker. I'm a country bumpkin. I was the vehicle. He had the gas. It's a great team, and I'm a big team player.

—REBA MCENTIRE, SINGER,
ON HUSBAND NARVEL BLACKSTOCK

The typical thing for a guy is to be really strong and capable, but then they have that other . . . feminine side, too. I like a mix.

—MARISA TOMEI, ACTOR

He was so brave. In the twenty-first century, a woman doesn't often see her knight fend off a real dragon.

—SHARON STONE, ACTOR, WHEN HUSBAND
PHIL BRONSTEIN WAS BITTEN BY A KOMODO DRAGON

I know this sounds ridiculous, but I like guys with love handles. I hate a washboard stomach.

—TARA REID, ACTOR

He's gorgeous, talented, supermacho. Give me macho or give me death!

—MADONNA, SINGER, ON HUSBAND GUY RITCHIE

Guy's-Eye View

The four things that I look for in a wife are character, intelligence, personality and beauty. And you have them all.

—MARTIN LUTHER KING, JR., CIVIL RIGHTS LEADER,
1929–1968, TO FUTURE WIFE CORETTA SCOTT

It's a big advantage to be with someone who is smart. She's not afraid to express her opinion, even though it is not always what I want to hear. I have enough people around me who are yes-people.

—ARNOLD SCHWARZENEGGER, ACTOR

Romantic Lyrics

Show me one man who knows his own heart
To him I shall belong

—JEWEL, SINGER-SONGWRITER

FASCINATING FACT

In a lovestories.com poll asking people what attracted them to their partners, forty-six percent said personality, while twenty-one percent said looks.

Chapter 25

The Last Word on Love

 Congratulations! You've come to the end of *The Girls' Book of Love*. All that's left now is for you to begin living—or at least imagining—your own love stories. Celebrate your crushes, delight in your dreams, and proceed into the landscape of love. May you find satisfying romantic connections and gratifying experiences beyond your wildest hopes and dreams!

Cool Quote

The heart is a living museum. In each of its galleries, no matter how narrow or dimly lit, preserved forever like wondrous diatoms, are our moments of loving and being loved.

—DIANE ACKERMAN, WRITER

Guy's-Eye View

In our life there is a single color, as on an artist's palette, which provides the meaning of life and art. It is the color of love.

—MARC CHAGALL, ARTIST, 1887–1985

Other Books about Love

HE'S NOT ALL THAT!: HOW TO ATTRACT THE GOOD GUYS, by Dr. Gilda Carle (Cliff Street Books, 2000)

A SMART GIRL'S GUIDE TO BOYS: SURVIVING CRUSHES, STAYING TRUE TO YOURSELF, AND OTHER STUFF, by Nancy Holyoke (Pleasant Co., 2001)

ROMANTIC BREAKUP: IT'S NOT THE END OF THE WORLD, by Jennifer Rozines Roy (Enslow, 2000)

THE GIRL'S GUIDE TO GUYS: STRAIGHT TALK FOR TEENS ON FLIRTING, DATING, BREAKING UP, MAKING UP & FINDING TRUE LOVE, by Julie Taylor (Three Rivers Press, 2000)

Resources: Troubled Relationships

In Love and in Danger: A Teen's Guide to Breaking Free of Abusive Relationships, by Barrie Levy (Seal Press, 1998)

Everything You Need to Know about Relationship Violence, by Katherine White (Rosen, 2001)

The 24-hour National Domestic Violence Hotline, (800) 799-7233, provides referrals.

The National Organization for Victim Assistance, (800) 879-6682 or (202) 232-6682; www.try-nova.org/for_victims_survivors.html. Provides info and referrals.

Copyright Acknowledgments

Kamalika Baral: "A Gift from the Gods" by Kamalika Baral. Copyright by Kamalika Baral. Reprinted by permission of the author; Jennifer Bernstein-Lewis: "Matchmaker Moms & Dads" by Jennifer Bernstein-Lewis. Copyright by Jennifer Bernstein-Lewis. Reprinted by permission of the author; Jessica Bettencourt: "Heart of Darkness" by Jessica Bettencourt. Copyright by Jessica Bettencourt. Reprinted by permission of the author; Kristin Bluhm: "Puppy Love" by Kristin Bluhm. Copyright by Kristin Bluhm. Reprinted by permission of the author; Eleanor Bron: "I waited/For the phone to ring . . ." by Eleanor Bron. Reprinted from *The Pillow Book of Eleanor Bron*. Copyright by Eleanor Bron; Muriel Calegari: "Special Delivery" by Muriel Calegari. Copyright by Muriel Calegari. Reprinted by permission of the author; Elizabeth Carlassare: "Beautiful Music" by Elizabeth Carlassare. Copyright by Elizabeth Carlassare. Reprinted by permission of the author; Dina Chehata: "Sneaking Up on Love" by Dina Chehata. Copyright by Dina Chehata. Reprinted by permission of the author; Andi Chrisman: "12 A.M." by Andi Chrisman. Copyright by Andi Chrisman. Reprinted by permission of the author; Terri Dale: "Engagement Rink" by Terri Dale. Copyright by Terri Dale. Reprinted by permission of the author; Tamra Dawn: "The Art of Knowing" by Tamra Dawn. Tamra Dawn is the pen name of Ruth Mason, an award-winning journalist. Copyright by The WholeFamily Center, Inc. Reprinted by permission of WholeFamily.com; Alden Dean: "For Better or Worse" by Alden Dean. Copyright by Alden Dean.

Reprinted by permission of the author; Gretchen Dean: "Up on the Roof" by Gretchen Dean. Copyright by Gretchen Dean. Reprinted by permission of the author; Ani DiFranco: "i'm sorry i can't help you . . ." by Ani DiFranco. Copyright 1994 by Righteous Babe Music. Reprinted by permission of Righteous Babe Music; Susan Fridkin: "Soul Mate" by Susan Fridkin. Copyright by Susan Fridkin. Reprinted by permission of the author; Camryn Green: "A Lesson in Love" by Camryn Green. Camryn Green is the pen name of Sherri Lederman Mandell, an author, humorist, and family commentator. Copyright by The WholeFamily Center, Inc. Reprinted by permission of Whole-Family.com; CJ Heck: "I Am" by CJ Heck. Copyright by CJ Heck. Reprinted by permission of the author; Sandra Jackson: "Attic Treasures" by Sandra Jackson. Copyright by Sandra Jackson. Reprinted by permission of the author; Courtney Jones: "The Love Monster" by Courtney Jones. Copyright by Courtney Jones. Reprinted by permission of the author; Jessica Litwin: "Better Shop Around" by Jessica Litwin. Copyright by Jessica Litwin. Reprinted by permission of the author; Sarah Longaker: "Lost and Found" by Sarah Longaker. Copyright by Sarah Longaker. Reprinted by permission of the au-thor; Nancy MacGregor: "A Sweet Story" by Nancy MacGregor. Copyright by Nancy MacGregor. Reprinted by permission of the author; Michelle Ghilotti Mandel: "The Book of Love" by Michelle Ghilotti Mandel. Copyright by Michelle Ghilotti Mandel. Reprinted by permission of the author; Sarah Maurice: "Light at the End of the Tunnel" by Sarah Maurice. Copyright by Sarah Maurice. Reprinted by permission of the author; Eve Merriam: "When" by Eve Merriam. Copyright 1993 by Eve Merriam. Reprinted by permission of

Marian Reiner; Ellen Birkett Morris: "Checking Him Out" by Ellen Birkett Morris. Copyright by Ellen Birkett Morris. Reprinted by permission of the author; Julie Niece: "A Good Sport" by Julie Niece. Copyright by Julie Niece. Reprinted by permission of the author; Janet O'Neal: "Quick Quiz: Are You Too Dependent?" from *Cracking the Love Code* by Janet O'Neal. Copyright by Janet O'Neal. Reprinted by permission of Broadway Books, a division of Random House, Inc.; Parade Publications: "Love Building Tactics" and "Relationship Rules According to Teens." Copyright © 2001 by *Parade*. Reprinted from column by Lynn Minton on March 11, 2001. Reprinted by permission of *Parade*. "Snow White and the Seven Years" adapted from quote by Kate Beckinsale in story by Tom Seligson in *Parade*, May 20, 2001. Copyright © 2001 *Parade*. Reprinted by permission of *Parade*; Maria Peevey: "Not in the Cards" by Maria Peevey. Copyright by Maria Peevey. Reprinted by permission of *Marie Claire*; Krista Quesenberry: "No Interest? No Problem" by Krista Quesenberry. Copyright by Krista Quesenberry. Reprinted by permission of the author; Lyndsay Rawle: "Moment of Truth" by Lyndsay Rawle. Copyright by Lyndsay Rawle. Reprinted by permission of the author; Helene Marie Rose: "I'd Love You If Only" by Helene Marie Rose. Copyright by Helene Marie Rose. Reprinted by permission of the author; Rosalie Rung: "Express Mail" by Rosalie Rung. Copyright by Rosalie Rung. Reprinted by permission of the author; Bonnie Sandler: "Give Me a Break!" by Bonnie Sandler. Copyright by Bonnie Sandler. Reprinted by permission of the author; Jennifer Schwarz: "Ahoy, (Room) Mate" by Jennifer Schwarz. Copyright by Jennifer Schwarz. Reprinted by permission of the author; Melissa Sisler: "A Good Deal at the Mall" by Melissa Sisler. Copyright by

Melissa Sisler. Reprinted by permission of the author; Mona Tura: "A Love for All Seasons" by Mona Tura. Copyright by Mona Tura. Reprinted by permission of the author; Judith Viorst: "And Then the Prince Knelt Down and Tried to Put the Glass Slipper on Cinderella's Foot" from *If I Were in Charge of the World and Other Worries* by Judith Viorst. Reprinted by permission of Simon & Schuster and Lescher & Lescher; Alanna Webb: "Closing Doors" by Alanna Webb. Copyright by Alanna Webb. Reprinted by permission of the author.

Index

Bob Houser

Catherine Dee's mission is to empower and inspire girls in all facets of their lives. In addition to this book, she's written *The Girls' Book of Friendship*, *The Girls' Book of Wisdom*, and *The Girls' Guide to Life*. Catherine lives in the San Francisco Bay Area and speaks to groups around the country.

You can reach her via www.deebest.com; cate@deebest.com; or regular mail care of Megan Tingley Books, Little, Brown and Company, 1271 Avenue of the Americas, New York, NY 10020.

Don't miss:

The Girls' Book of Friendship

"An inspiring collection." — *Publishers Weekly*

"Girls will return to its pages again and again when they are looking for just the right words to say 'thanks,' a bit of inspiration, and practical advice as well."

— *School Library Journal*

The Girls' Book of Wisdom

An ALA Popular Paperback for Young Adults and a Quick Pick for Reluctant Young Adult Readers

A winner of the Disney Adventures Best Book Award

"This collection is upbeat and lighthearted. . . . The handy size combined with the accessible format will appeal to this age group."

— *School Library Journal*

"*The Girls' Book of Wisdom* features quotes from a dynamic group of intelligent women. Each idea has something positive to offer girls."

— Ann Richards, former governor of Texas

The Girls' Guide to Life

A *San Francisco Chronicle Book Review* "Best Bet," 1997

"*The Girls' Guide to Life* is like having a best girlfriend for every activity you can think of. . . . A friendly, commonsense approach for girls who are learning and exploring the basics of life." —Gloria Steinem

"Fact-packed and thought-provoking . . . a pleasing and valuable guide."

—*Kirkus*